You Can Do It...
Play BASS!

Matt Scharfglass

AMSCO PUBLICATIONS
part of The Music Sales Group

London / New York /
Paris / Sydney / Copenhagen / Berlin /
Madrid / Tokyo

This book © Copyright 2009 by
Amsco Publications.
Music © Copyright 2009
Dorsey Brothers Music Limited.
All Rights Reserved.
International Copyright Secured.

Exclusive Distributors:

Music Sales Corporation
257 Park Avenue South
New York, NY 10010, USA

Music Sales Limited
14-15 Berners Street
London W1T 3LJ, UK

Music Sales Pty. Limited
20 Resolution Drive,
Caringbah, NSW 2229, Australia

Order No. AM991210
ISBN 13: 978.0.8256.3579.3

Written by Matt Scharfglass.
Edited by Tom Fleming.
Designed by Michael Bell Design.
Music processed by Paul Ewers Music Design.
Illustrations by Andy Hammond.
Photography by George Taylor.
Modeled by Jonas Persson & Tom Fleming.
Aria IGB Bass courtesy of Scott Avery at
Music Ground Limited.
Printed in the U.S.A. by Vicks Lithograph.

ABOUT THE AUTHOR

Guitar World music editor **Matt Scharfglass** has performed around the country and internationally, playing virtually all types of music with a wide range of artists, including R&B with Ashford and Simpson, old-school swing with the Blue Saracens and gospel with Richard Hartley & Soul Resurrection. Matt appears on the original-cast recording of *Evil Dead: The Musical* and the Broadway Cares album *Home for the Holidays*. He has also worked in countless theater pits and plays guitar up in the organ booth to crowds of 18,000 at Rangers home games at Madison Square Garden.

An accomplished guitar and bass transcriber, Matt has had more than 600 of his transcriptions appear in *Guitar World* magazine and in books by Warner Brothers, Music Sales and Hal Leonard. He has also authored more than a dozen bass and guitar instructional books, including *Beginning Blues Bass, Starting Guitar: The Number One Method For Young Guitarists, How To Tune Your Guitar,* and *The Gig Bag Book Of Practical Pentatonics*. He currently is the bassist and one of the main songwriters for his rock band, the Border Cops.

Thanks...
This book could never have happened without:
The support and encouragement of Ed Lozano, Peter Pickow and Dan Earley at Music Sales.
The understanding of Jimmy Brown at *Guitar World*.
The love and patience of my beautiful wife, Sandra Dubrov.

CD Acknowledgements
Narration by Paul Vassallo.
All music composed and performed by Matt Scharfglass.

CD TRACK LIST

CD 1

SLOW ROCK GROOVES

MID-TEMPO ROCK GROOVES

REGGAE & SKA GROOVES

USING THIS BOOK

I recently read an article in a musician's magazine written by a relatively unknown recording session bassist. He had been invited to a three-day gathering of bass players from all over the world, during which several famous bassists were scheduled to play in featured solo performances. To his delight he had also been asked to perform.

Figuring he'd come up with something to play when he got there, he didn't stress out about it too much; this was of course before he witnessed the first bass player of the evening. He recalled with terror this musician's blinding speed, proficiency in slapping and two-handed tapping and overall stunning technique and showmanship. Each bassist that followed only outperformed the one before, consistently bringing the audience to its feet.

With thoughts of "I'm a dead man" coursing through his head, it was his turn to take the stage. After plugging into the amp and surveying the rapt audience, he did the only thing he could do at the moment: he played bass.

No slapping. No popping. No two-handed tapping gymnastics. Just big, fat, glorious bass *grooves* played with big, fat, glorious *tone* and *attitude*.

I'm as awed by stunning technique as the next guy. But when it comes right down to it, all it really takes to connect with an audience is a big fat groove. What does this have to do with this book? You've tinkered with the bass; perhaps you became quite good at it, but it got pushed to the side over the years. Or maybe you simply didn't get very far with it and became frustrated and uninterested. Either way, this is the book for you. Whatever your story, my goal is to have you spinning off booty-shaking grooves in as little time (and with as little hair loss) as possible. While this book assumes you have some basic musical knowledge, don't sweat the reading part of it too much; with the CD, you can hear the musical examples and play along. This book is to be *played*, not studied; you will not be bogged down with theory.

My only suggestion before beginning is to have your bass examined and set up for maximum playability by a professional guitar technician. I've seen many guitar and bass students give up quickly under the misconception that they have no musical ability whatsoever, when in reality the instruments they were playing were simply in terrible condition.

That said, I hope you enjoy the music offered in this book. I think the best way to learn to play is to, well, *play*, so let's get to it.

TECHNIQUE BASICS

TECHNIQUE BASICS

RELAX...

In spite of everything you
may have been told by
teachers about correct
posture, hand position, etc.,
there are actually as many
ways to hold and play the
bass as there are players:
sitting down, standing up,
lying down...

...the most important
thing is that you should feel
comfortable. Relax.

I SAID RELAX!

LEFT HAND

Classical guitar technique says that your left hand should stay "anchored" to the middle of the neck.

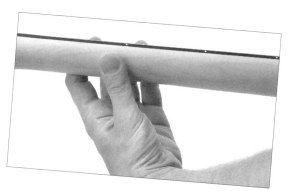

Rock players, particularly on the heavier side of things, frequently bring their thumb way up over the top of the neck. This is not the end of the world, unless you want to play fierce jazz solos in the manner of John Pattitucci.

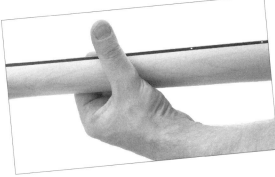

Letting your thumb stray below the center line, or off sideways, is generally not a good idea. It just doesn't give you the strength you need to keep those thick bass strings from buzzing.

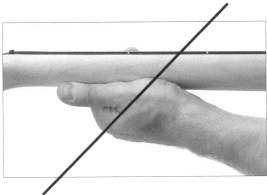

RIGHT HAND

"Textbook" right-hand technique uses the first two fingers of the right hand, alternating between the two. It is usually convenient to rest the thumb on the bottom string when playing the higher strings, on one of the pickups, or the end of the fretboard.

This position can easily be changed to accommodate *slap technique*, where the side of the thumb slaps the strings and the fingers pull or "pop" the upper strings for that punchy sound beloved of funk and disco players.

Note: Excessive use of this technique in your local music store will probably get you thrown out.

Rock players often use a pick, especially when playing "even" eighth notes. If you play guitar too, you'll probably find that you need a heavier gauge for playing bass.

So it's really up to you. Don't worry about it too much. If it feels comfortable, it's probably fine.

Pull up a chair, grab your preferred liquid refreshment, put the cat out, sit back and play bass!

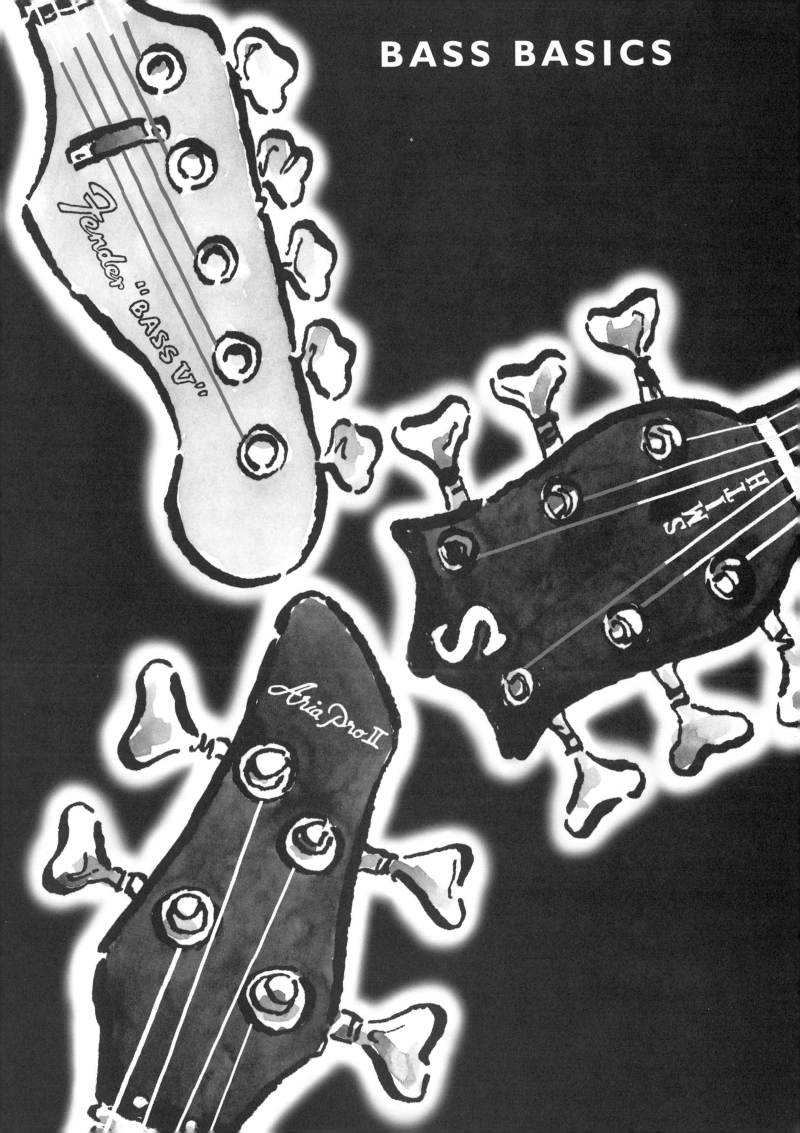

BASS BASICS

BASS BASICS

You may find this information useful for curiosity's sake or perhaps for making a decision on a new instrument purchase.

Four, Five, or Six Strings: Generally, a bass has four strings, tuned E-A-D-G from low to high.

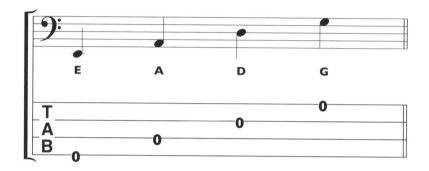

In the 1980s, five-string models began appearing on the market, featuring a low B string below the E.

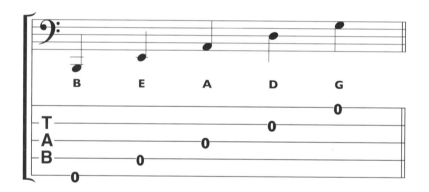

These were quickly followed by six-string models, which are tuned the same as the five-string with the addition of a C string above the G.

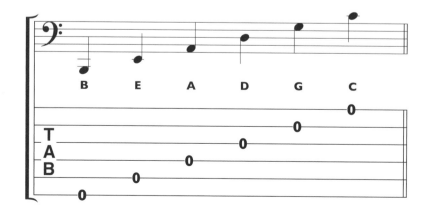

For the purposes of this book, we will focus only on the four-string variety as it is the most commonly used.

Fretted vs. Fretless: Most bass players favor fretted basses and own a fretless that they use occasionally. A few bassists, however, have chosen the fretless as their trademark—the late Jaco Pastorius being the most obvious example. Pino Palladino, while not exactly a household name, is another great fretless bassist whose skills have been sought after by artists such as Paul Young, Elton John, Pete Townshend, Don Henley, and countless others over the past twenty years.

The fretless bass has its own vibe; Jeff Berlin, a legend of the electric bass, has said he refuses to play fretless because there's no way to do it without sounding like Jaco, and if you're not going to excel on the instrument, you may as well not even bother with it. Of course, this is a matter of opinion. There's no doubt that the fretted bass is the more commonly used of the two, but some players find that they can express themselves with a fretless in ways not possible on a fretted bass, and vice versa.

Tone: There's an old musician's adage that states, "Tone is in the hands." I happen to agree with this sentiment: You can play through your favorite bass player's amp using his exact bass, but you'll never sound just like him, even if you play all the right notes. The way one plays an instrument, regardless of skill level, is an intensely personal thing.

That said, the actual physical locations where you pluck the strings make up a big part of your sound. If you pluck right near the bridge, your tone will be tight and punchy (Jaco again). As you pluck closer to the neck, the sound becomes duller and "thuddier"; think Black Sabbath—in some songs, you can actually hear Geezer Butler's aggressive plucking-hand technique causing the strings to hit the pickup.

Another component in your sound is your pickup configuration. Most basses have two pickups: one located near the neck, and the other located near the bridge. If you want a sharp, punchy tone *à la* Jaco, the bridge pickup is the way to go. If you're more of a funk/traditional rock person, you'll want to go with the neck pickup for a deeper, "mid-rangier" tone.

Most basses, by way of a pickup switch, let you dial in each pickup separately or a combination of the two. Between your pickups, the tone controls on the bass, and where you pluck the string, you have plenty of tonal options available to you before the signal even reaches the amp.

EH, NOT SO FAST, JUNIOR

Sorry, but you're going to have to tune up that thing before you turn up that thing. This is purely optional of course, but it's probably a wise move to be in tune with the accompanying CD if you're planning on playing along with it (unless you're deliberately going for that trashy, devil-may-care Johnny Thunders or Sid Vicious vibe).

I've provided reference pitches on Tracks 1 through 4 of the CD. Since each pitch is on its own track, you can set your CD player to repeat the track so you'll have as much time as you need to tune the string.

Track 1

E TUNING NOTE

Track 2

A TUNING NOTE

Track 3

D TUNING NOTE

Track 4

G TUNING NOTE

READY TO ROCK?

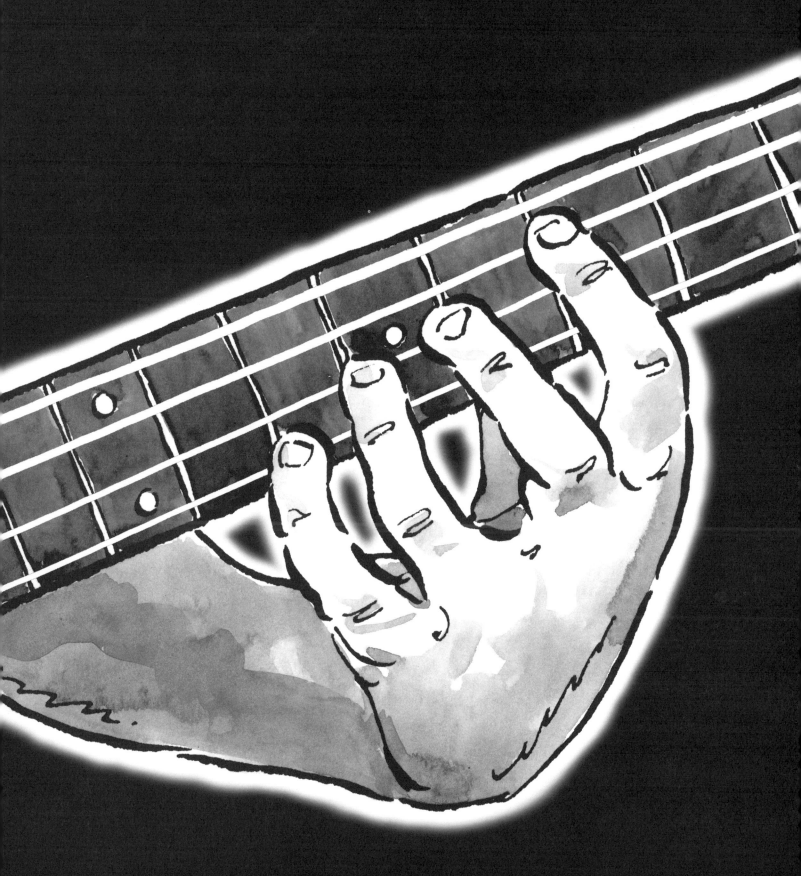

NOTHING BUT GROOVES

Before we begin, with your indulgence I'd like to put forward my take on the number-one rule of bass:

All bass playing, regardless of musical style, is about attitude, groove, and tone. Speed and fancy techniques are secondary.

Fortunately, rock-solid playing doesn't require much technique. If you can keep a steady tempo (very important!) and play what you are able to play with conviction, you're already halfway there. The grooves you'll find in these pages are so simple to play, yet so effective, people will think you've been playing far longer than you actually have.

Remember: Play with an attitude! Let's begin.

ROCK

SLOW ROCK GROOVES

We'll start off with a couple of simple, open-string grooves. Concentrate on locking in with the drums and creating a strong, steady backdrop.

SLOW 145

**CD I
TRACK 5**

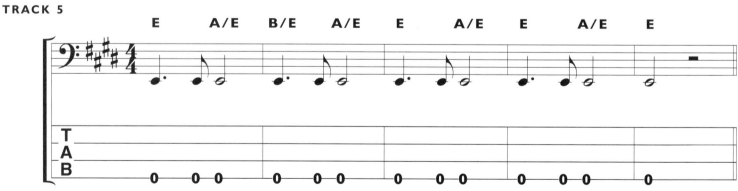

22

Be sure to deaden the low E string with your fretting hand when you move to the open A in the third bar of this next one.

THE ADDED SUSPENSE IS KILLING ME

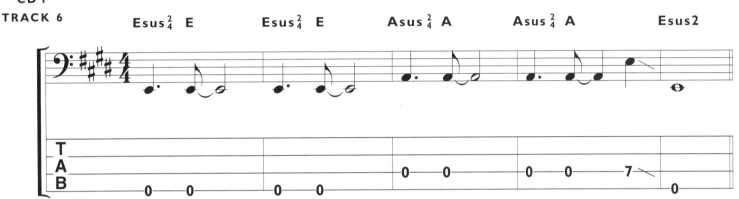

Though this groove involves fretted notes, the whole thing is played on one string.

WE'VE GOT ALL YEAR

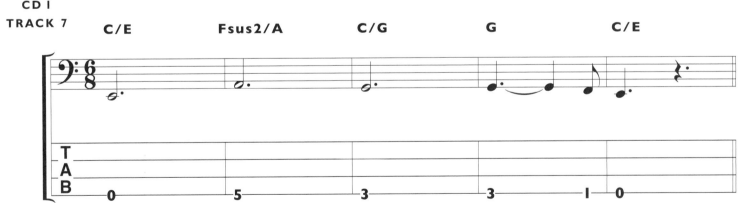

In the next two grooves, take care not to cut any notes off too early; hold each one for its entire duration.

PÖWER BÄLLAD

SUSPENDED WITHOUT PAY

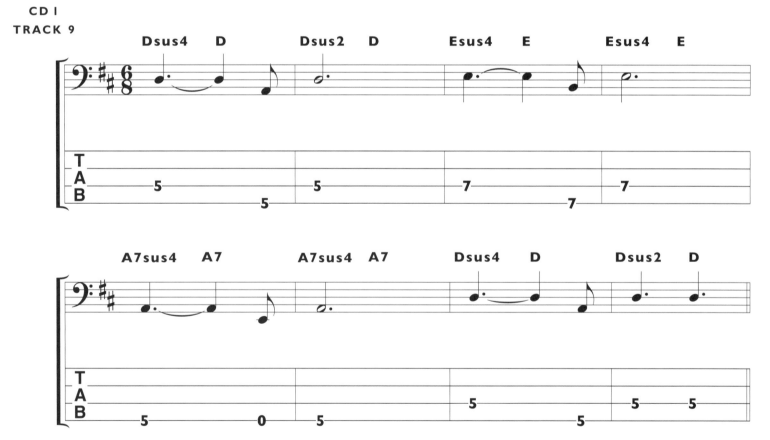

"Steely Shoes": *Note the staccato marking (.) above the third beat in every measure; this means to make the note short.*

24

STEELY SHOES

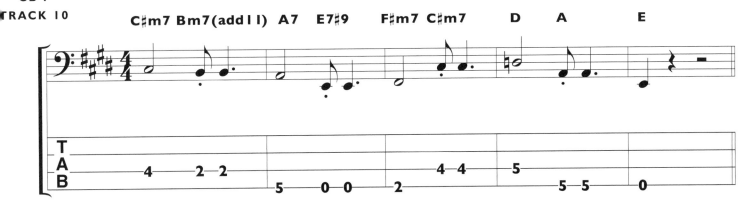

"Adrian! Adrian!" uses a simple, straight-eighth-note groove under a common chord progression.

ADRIAN! ADRIAN!

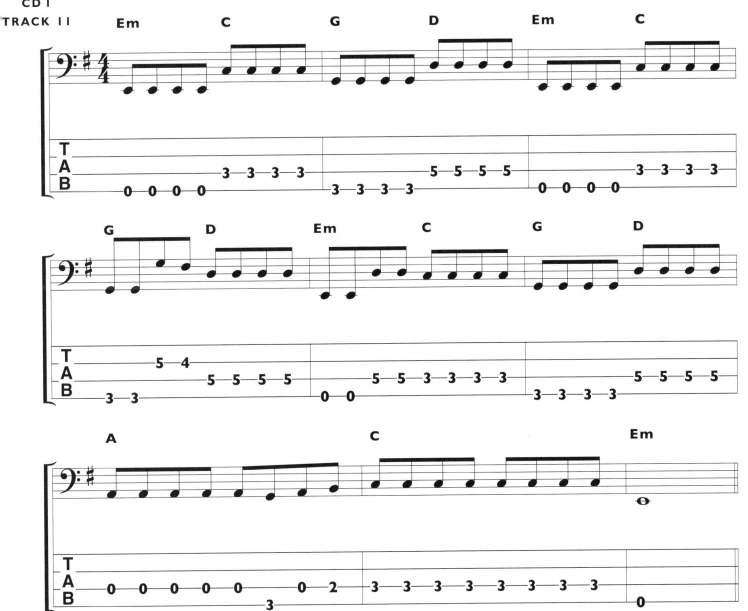

These last two grooves feature syncopated rhythms. As always, the interplay between the bass and drums should be tight.

STRAIGHT TO VIDEO

CD 1
TRACK 12

SAVE THE DRAMA FOR YOUR MAMA

CD 1
TRACK 13

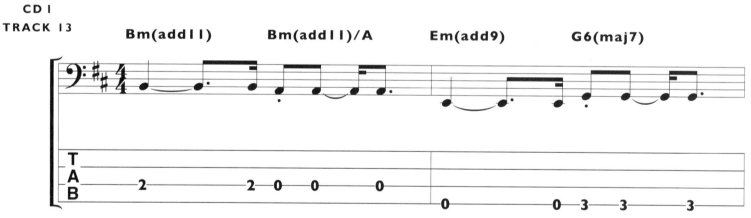

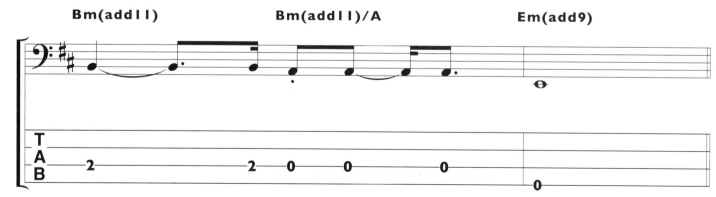

MID-TEMPO ROCK GROOVES

In this section you'll find bass lines that run the gamut from 1950s-style rock and roll to modern rock.

Let's start with a really easy one. Sometimes, a single note is all that's required for a bass line. When there are different chords being played over it (by the guitarist, for instance), having the same note anchoring the bottom end throughout the entire musical phrase can actually make for powerful results.

MY CAMARO

CD 1
TRACK 14

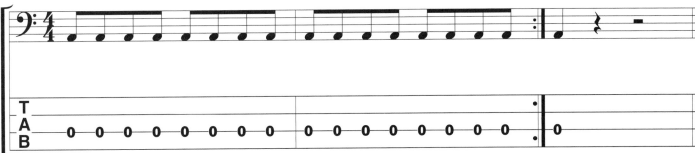

This one's a simple two-note phrase. Note the falloff on the very last note… instant rock credibility!

THESE JAZZ CHORDS ROCK

CD 1
TRACK 15

The next six grooves feature notes that are all played on the same string; simply shift or slide up or down to get to whichever note you need.

HE ALWAYS KEPT A FULLY STOCKED BARRE

HIDE THE GLITTER, HERE COMES ZIGGY

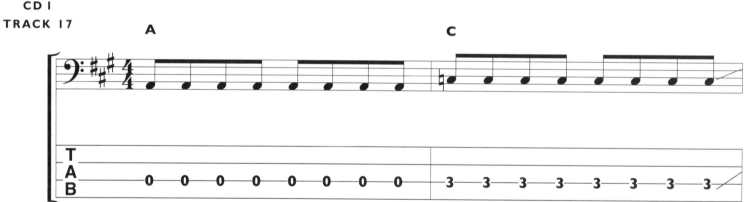

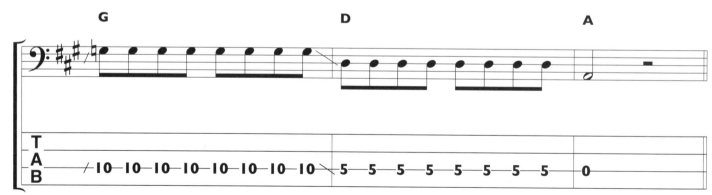

28

IT'S LIKE DÉJÀ VU ALL OVER AGAIN

CD 1
TRACK 18

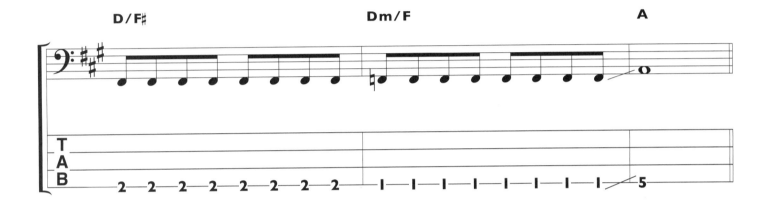

CALIPUNK

CD 1
TRACK 19

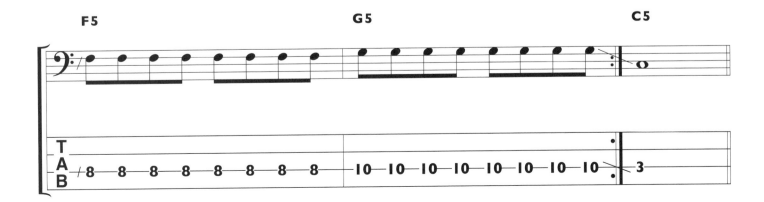

POWDER POP

CD I
TRACK 20

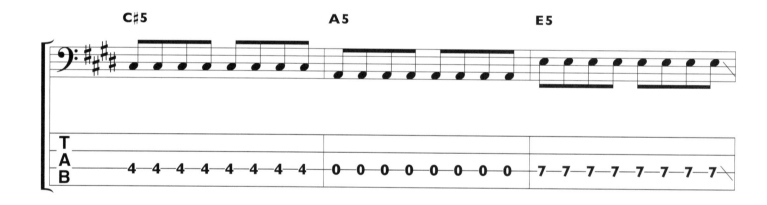

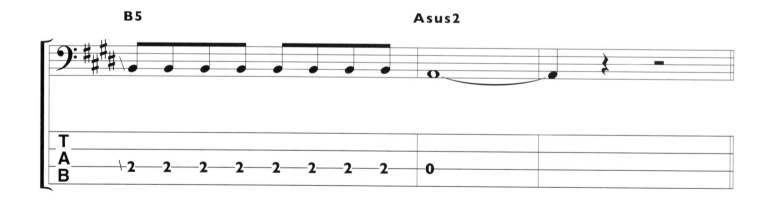

I lied (a little). This groove is also played entirely on the same string, except for the seventh bar, which features a "Hey Joe" type of climb.

WHERE DID I PUT THOSE MAJESTIC SUPERSONIC PUMPKINS?

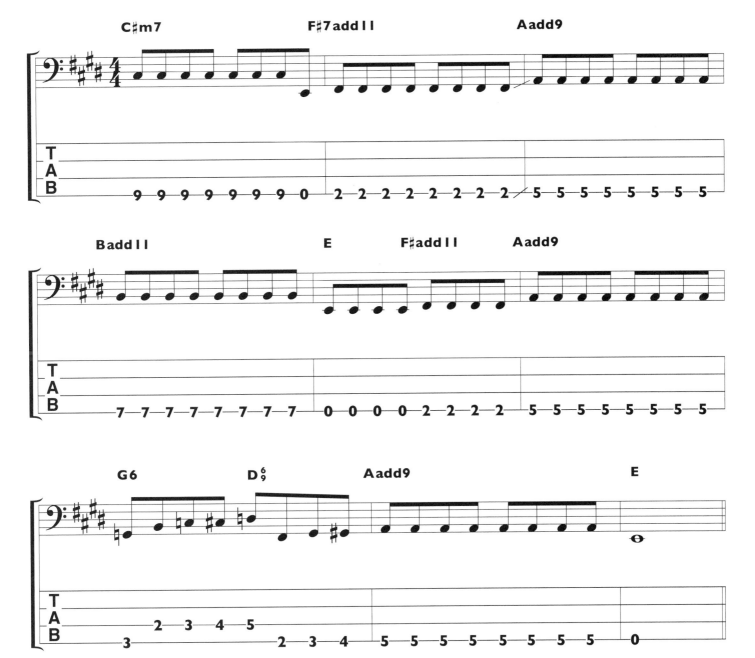

For the next handful of grooves, we'll touch on different types of rock feels and tempos.

CD 1
TRACK 22

MIRRORBALL

CD 1
TRACK 23

UMLAUTS ARE FÜN

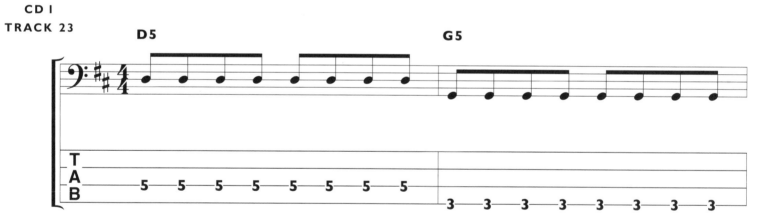

I USED TO LOVE PLAYING BASS

CD I

TRACK 24

CD I
TRACK 25

COUNTING JANGLES

CD I
TRACK 26

MORE THAN THE FEELING OF YOU
SHAKING ME ALL NIGHT LONG

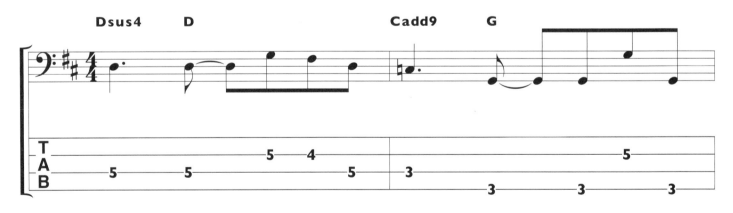

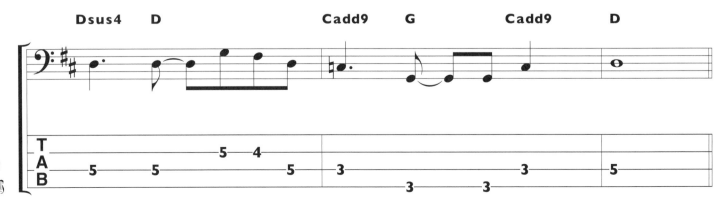

SMOOTH LIKE ME

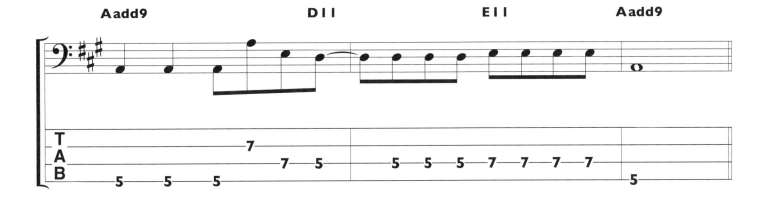

DON'T HAVE A COW

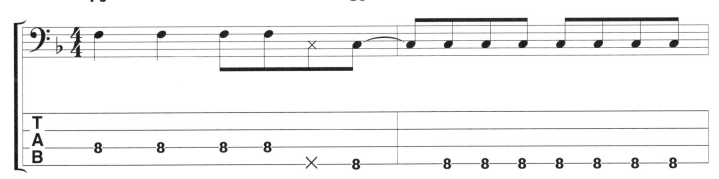

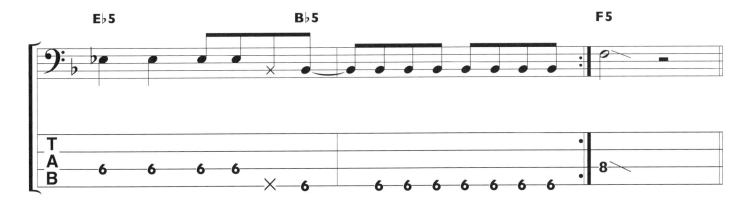

THE BOTTOM LINE

BAGEL WITH OX

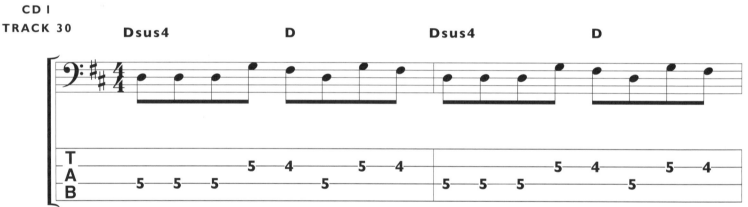

This next musical snippet makes use of an open string (the A string in this case) to anchor the groove while throwing in a couple of fretted notes.

GOT NO TIME

CD 1

TRACK 31

A7add11

Dig in and make each note count.

ALL THE PRETTY COLORS

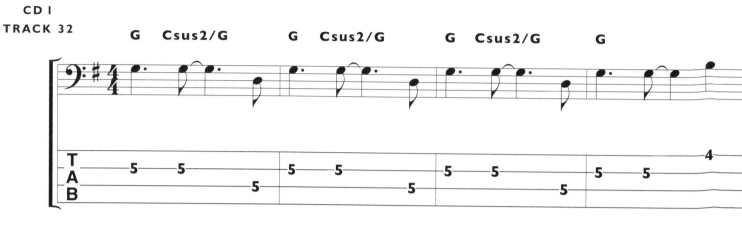

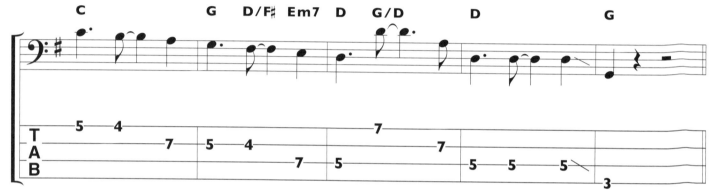

This one has a tricky fret-hand position shift in the second measure. Strive to hold out each note for its full duration and play the phrase as seamlessly as possible.

DUSTY CONVERTIBLE

Dig into each note for maximum heavy effect.

CD 1
TRACK 34

LOW END STOMP

This groove utilizes syncopated sixteenth notes for a slightly loose, funky feel.

CD 1
TRACK 35

YAWN... BORING... HEY, WAIT, THIS IS KIND OF COOL

Syncopated eighth notes make an appearance once again in this next example.

MOSH PIT IN THE DENTIST'S OFFICE

CD I
TRACK 36

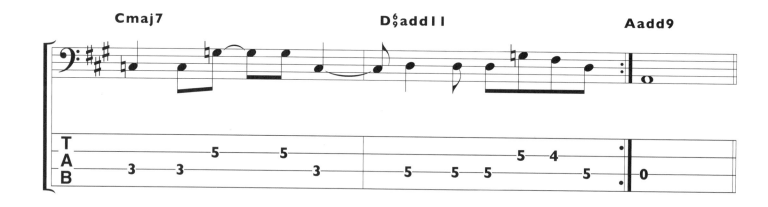

And now for a little fifties flavor…

POUTING IN THE CORNER AT THE SOCK HOP

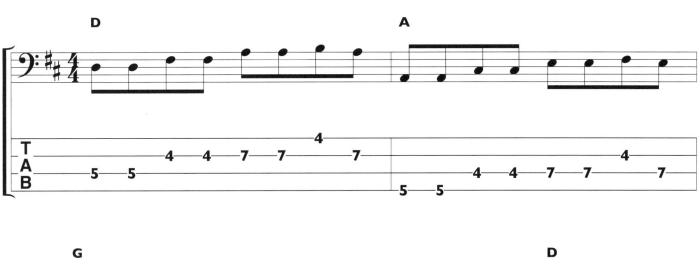

This melodic groove is played on the upper register of the instrument, which helps it jump right out of the mix.

CD 1
TRACK 38

GLAM GARAGE

Here are a couple of solid, classic-rock-oriented grooves.

LONG DISTANCE HAMMER-ON

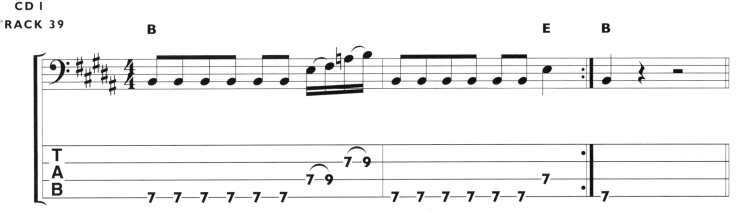

PURPLE BASS ALL IN MY BRAIN

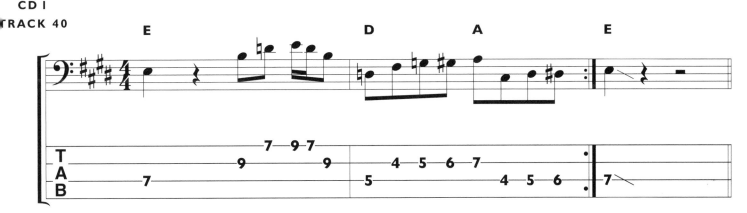

REGGAE & SKA GROOVES

Reggae bass is all about laying back, locking in tightly with the drums, and letting the groove rule. Add a few well-placed notes and you're well on your way.

STUFFED SPEEDO

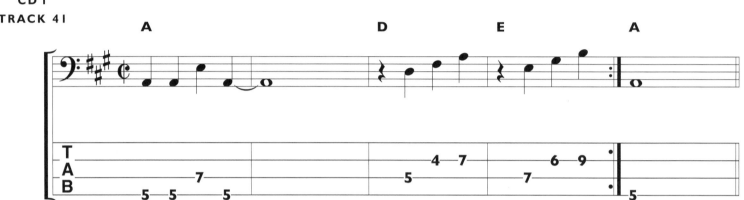

LAZY SKANKING

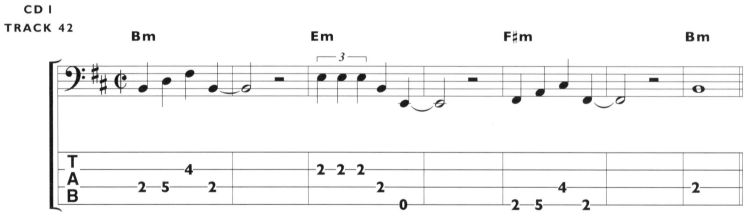

PUT DOWN THE CHEESE AND
STEP AWAY FROM THE BUFFET TABLE

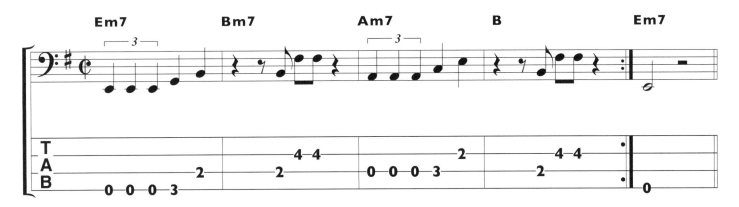

Ska is a somewhat amped-up version of reggae. You may notice that some of the grooves here are actually quite like some of the mid-tempo rock grooves we covered in the last section.

I WANNA BE A LIFEGUARD

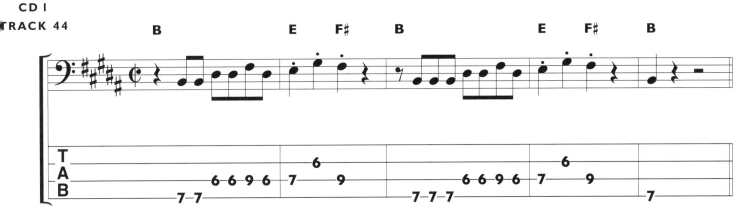

BASS CHASE

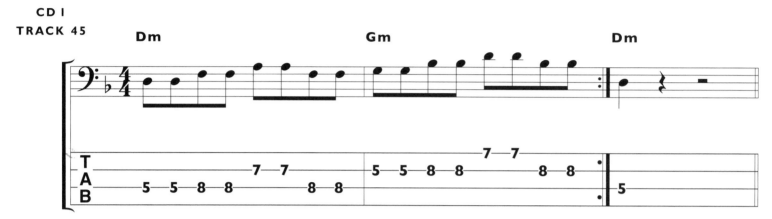

TOGA PARTY

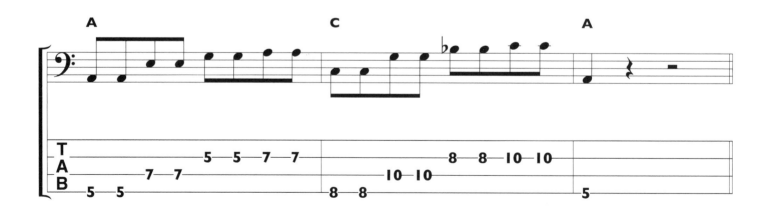

DISCO GROOVES

The role of the bass player in disco is to get people moving. Fortunately, a simple groove, even one punctuated with lots of space such as "Polyester Power" below, is all that is needed.

POLYESTER POWER

Straight, no-frills eighth-note grooves will often get the job done as well.

VELVET ROPE

BOUNCER BOOGIE

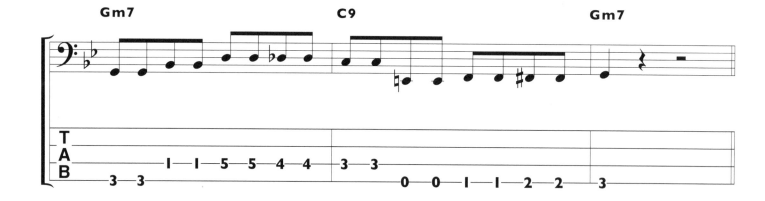

Just as straight-eighth-note lines are part and parcel of the rock bass idiom, energetic eighth-note octave grooves such as the one in the following musical example are standard in the disco format.

Be sure to hold each note out for its full duration (no choppiness) and play the line as smoothly as possible.

GET 'EM, PONCH

CD I

TRACK 50

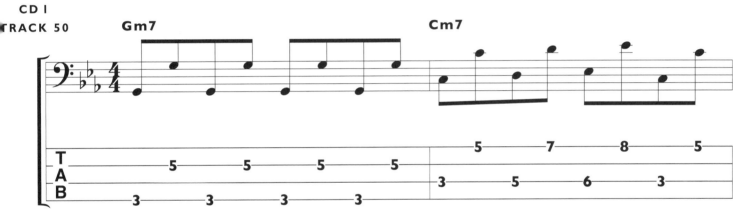

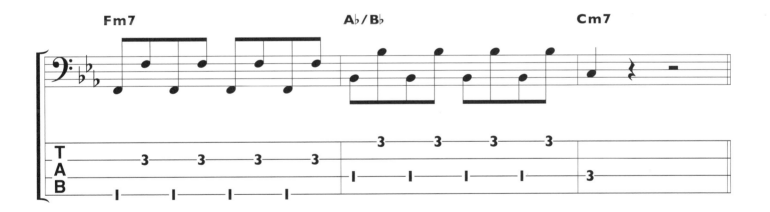

This one uses deadened notes for a percussive effect. To do this, simply lift your fret-hand finger off the fingerboard but maintain contact with the string.

SHAKE MY WHAT?

CD 1
TRACK 51

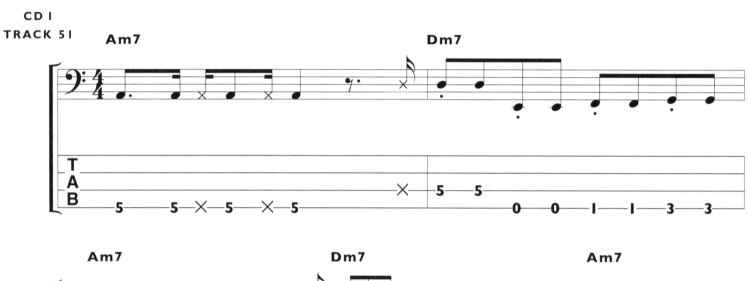

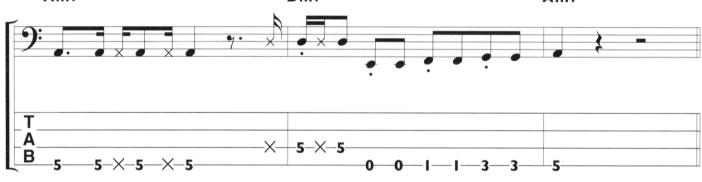

This groove also uses muted notes for percussive effect, and is especially useful for a breakdown or solo in the middle of a song. It is a little tricky at first, so if it gives you any trouble, just practice it slowly and run through it a few times until you get the feel of it under your fingers.

Many times, mastering a tricky technique is simply a matter of training your hand muscles to "remember" where to go.

GIVE THE BASS PLAYER SOME

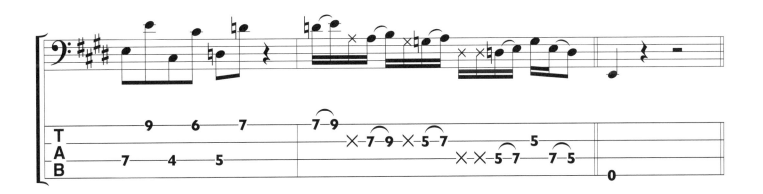

R&B GROOVES

We'll begin this section with a slow, slinky, smooth rhythm-and-blues ballad groove. Remember to make each note count and play with an attitude!

CD I
TRACK 53

AIN'T NOTHIN' RHYMES WITH "AMONGST"

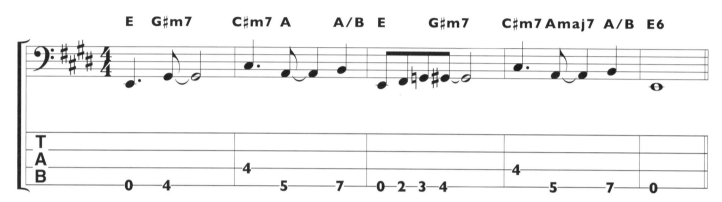

This simple Curtis Mayfield-style groove uses syncopated eighth notes.

CD I
TRACK 54

NOONTIME TRAIN TO JERSEY

Kick it old school!

HEY OTIS

HEY BABY, WHERE'D YOU PUT MY THANG

MUSTANG ALFIE (PART 1)

The bass is what drives the next couple of grooves. Step out into the spotlight and enjoy it!

BASS PLAYERS CAN'T DANCE

CD 1
TRACK 58

Let's wrap this up with a funky sixteenth-note romp.

GREASY TWINKIES

CD 1
TRACK 59

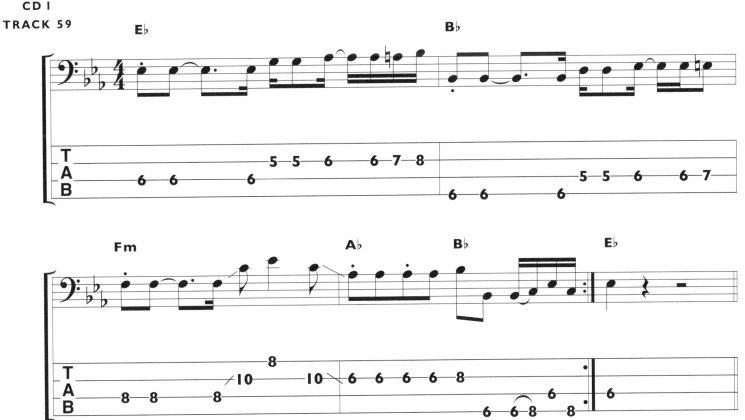

FUNK GROOVES

I had a friend, a fellow bass player, who landed a gig with a legendary, world-famous blind rhythm and blues pianist and singer. One day, during a rehearsal for an upcoming tour, this venerable entertainer called a funk tune. My friend, being very young, rather nervous, and eager to impress, launched into the most technical slapping and popping tricks he could muster. About a minute into the song, the boss stopped the band and said, "Bass player."

My friend, feeling rather satisfied with himself, replied, "Yes?"

"You're overplayin', [expletive deleted]," was the reply.

His gentle point being, of course, that funk is all about attitude and groove, not chops or slapping. My friend's showboating, while impressive, was getting in the way of the song. That said, let's begin this section with an easy single-note open-string groove.

By the way, I would recommend plucking the strings near the bridge, not just for this next musical example but also for every groove contained in this section.

**CD 1
TRACK 60**

POCKET MAN

The next two examples demonstrate how a few simple notes can deliver the funk as well as anything. Notice also how the rests, or spaces in between the notes, really make the notes stand out.

CD I
TRACK 61

KEVIN'S SEVENTH HEAVEN

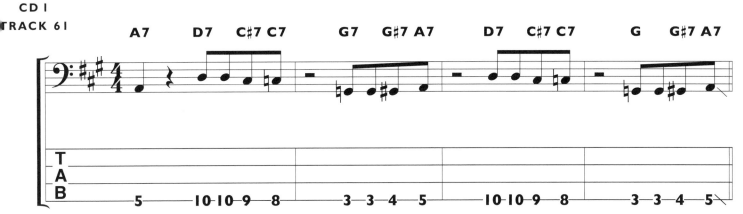

CD I
TRACK 62

GIVE THE CLARINET PLAYER SOME (BREAK IT DOWN!)

The next groove combines short, straight eighth notes with percussive deadened notes. The third and fourth bars are the same as the first two, except for some slight rhythmic variations. Note the random slide on the last beat of the fourth bar.

UH HUH

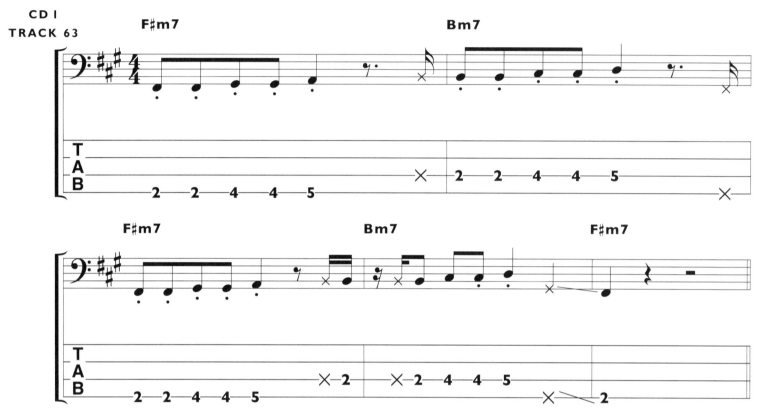

Let's get this party started...

AW YEAH

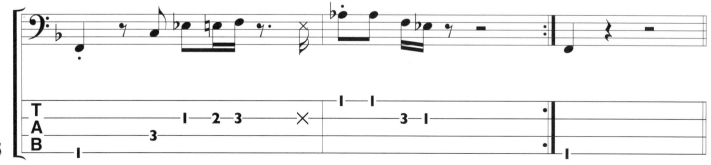

Here's an extremely funky and rather tricky one. All the muted notes are played on the A string.

As is the case with the other tricky examples in this book: If you run into any trouble, just practice it slowly and run through it a few times until you get the feel of it under your fingers.

Keep in mind that many times, mastering a tricky technique is simply a matter of training your hand muscles to "remember" where to go; this is simply a physical factor and not necessarily a reflection on your ability!

CD I
TRACK 65

UGH! YEAH! UH HUH

BLUES

The blues style is based on a standard twelve-bar chord progression commonly referred to as, well, a *blues progression*. Using the key of C for the sake of example, here is the general form (there are variations in every blues song):

- One bar of your starting chord **C**

- One bar of the "four" chord **F**

- Two bars of the starting chord **C**

- Two bars of the "four" chord **F**

- Two bars of the starting chord **C**

- One bar of the "five" chord **G**

- One bar of the "four" chord **F**

- Two bars of the starting chord **C**

Wait a minute, what do I mean by "four" chords and "five" chords? Well, since we're in the key of C, let's take a minute to review a **C Major Scale**.

C MAJOR SCALE

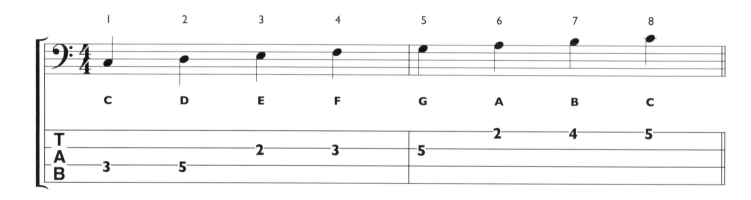

The note C is indicated as *1*. F is the fourth note from C, and G is the fifth note; thus their numerical indications *4* and *5*. Therefore, if C is the starting or "one" chord, F would be the "four" chord and G would be the "five."

Without further ado, we'll cover three different blues styles in this section: slow blues, funk blues, and shuffles.

SLOW BLUES

SAUSAGE FINGER BLUES

CD 1
TRACK 66

FUNK BLUES

MUSTANG ALFIE (PART 2)

CD 1
TRACK 67

CHUNKY FUNKIES

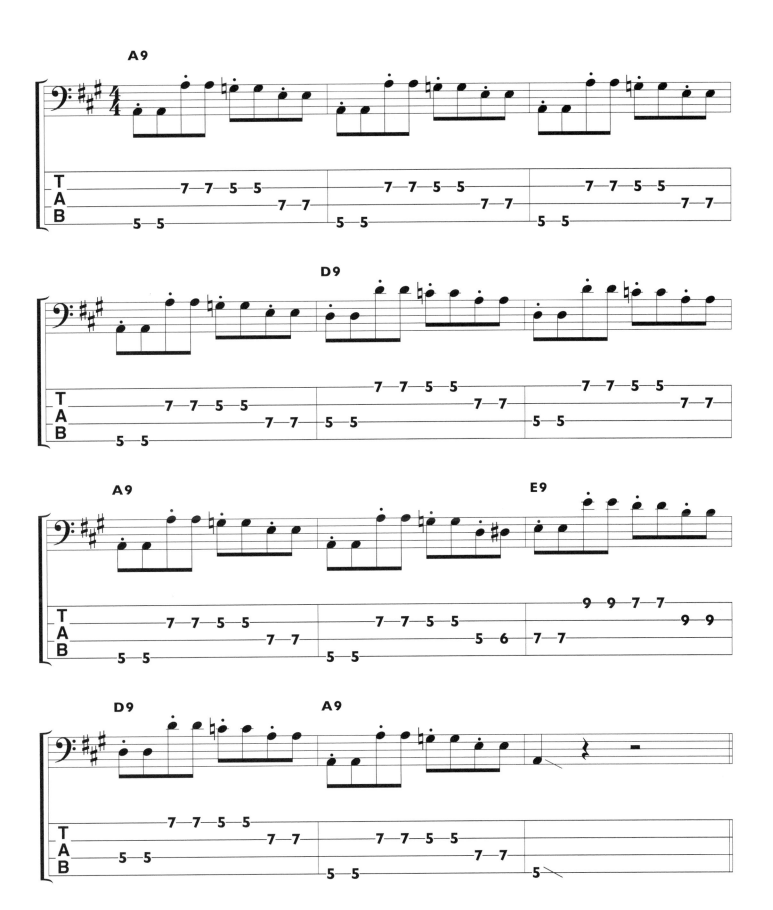

BLUES SHUFFLES

NASTY BLUES

CD I
TRACK 69

ROAD TRIP!

LATIN GROOVES

The feel of this first Latin groove is referred to as *bossa nova*.

MEET ME IN THE LOUNGE FOR COCKTAILS

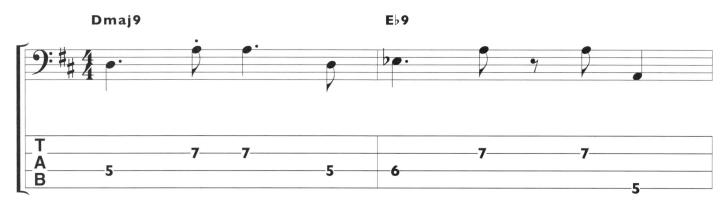

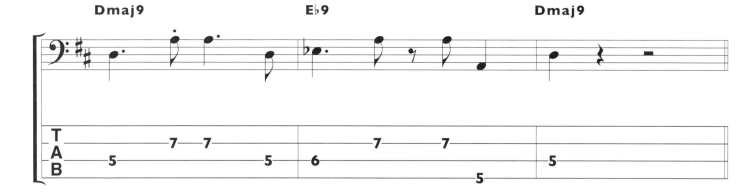

The next three grooves are examples of *samba*. This Latin style is generally played at faster tempos (compared to bossa novas). Notice the tied notes in "Bass Showgirl" and "Look, It's Montuno Boy."

BASS SHOWGIRL

CD 1
TRACK 72

LOOK, IT'S MONTUNO BOY

CD 1
TRACK 73

LIKE A BULL IN A CHINA SHOP

CD 1
TRACK 74

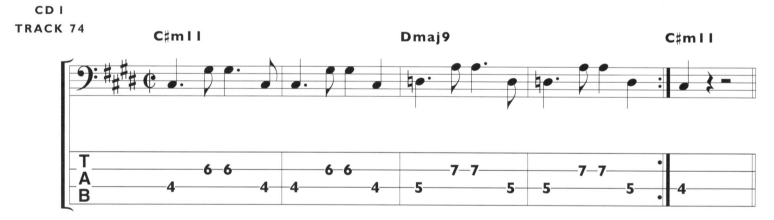

In recent years, Latin-influenced rock has been making some inroads into mainstream music.

LET'S GO BARRE-HOPPING

And finally, some calypso to kick back with.

CD 1
TRACK 76

GOING BANANAS

*What better way to close out this book than to put everything we've learned
into practice?*

*Throughout the following section, we'll cover three popular styles of music: reggae,
funk blues, and rock.*

Enjoy!

STYLES

CD I
TRACK 77

TIE-DYED PIZZA KEG

TRACK 78
Backing Track

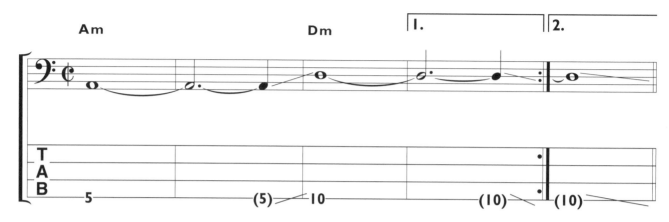

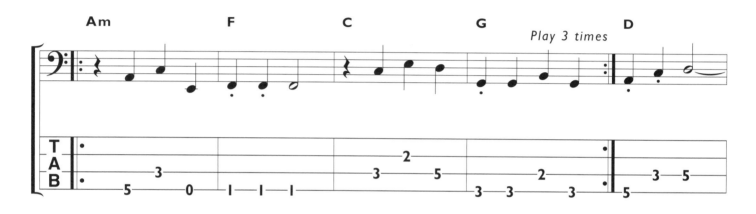

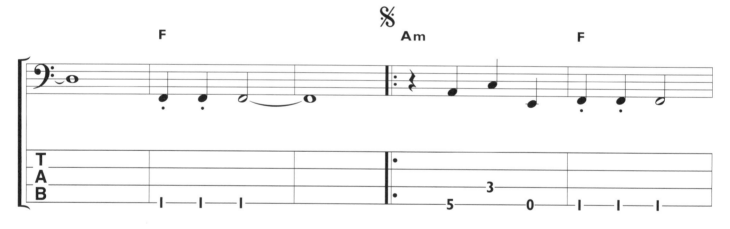

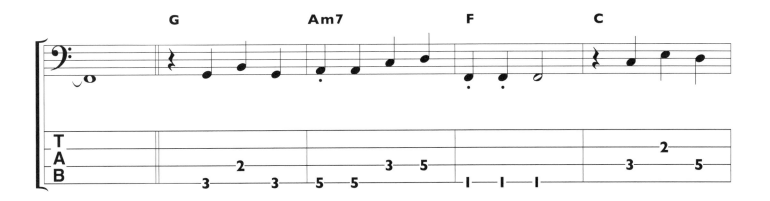
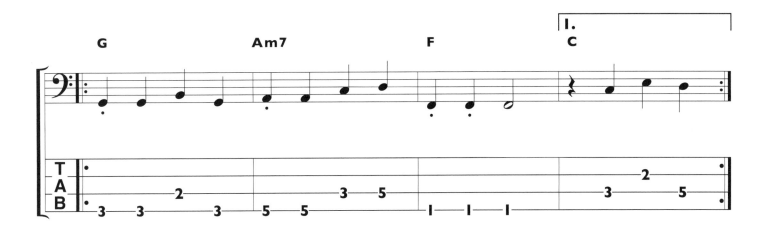
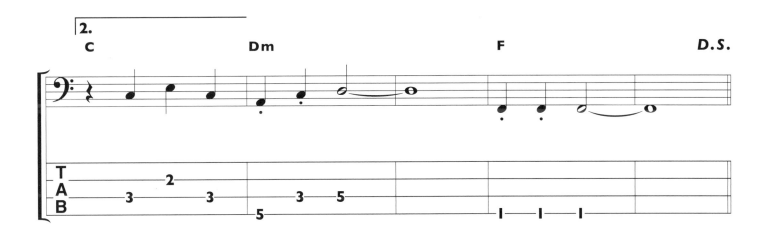
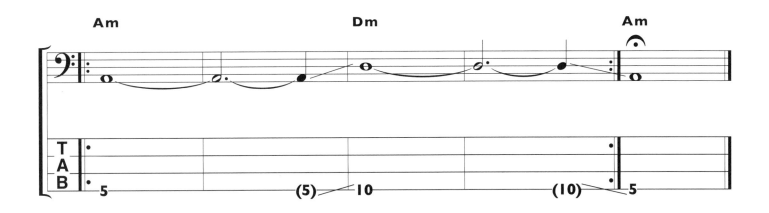

IT AIN'T GONNA FIT IN THERE

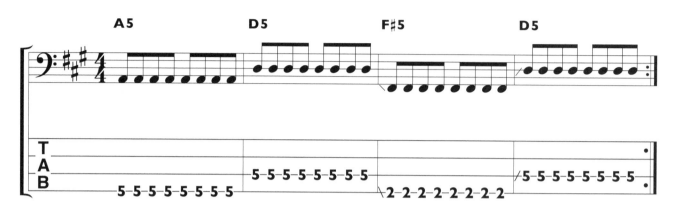

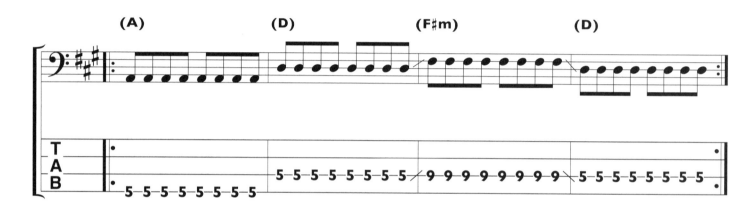

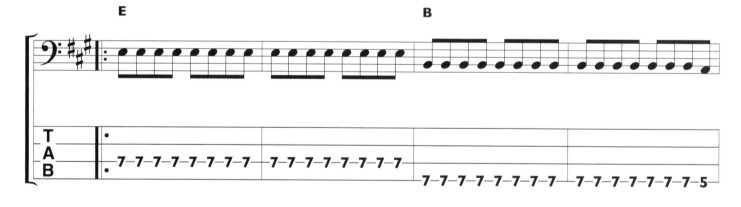

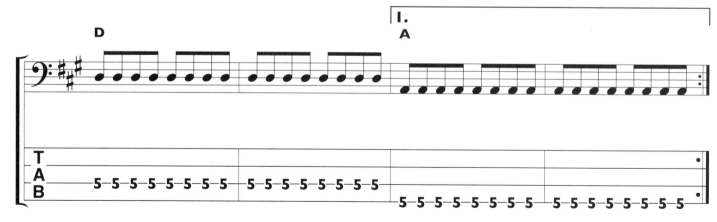

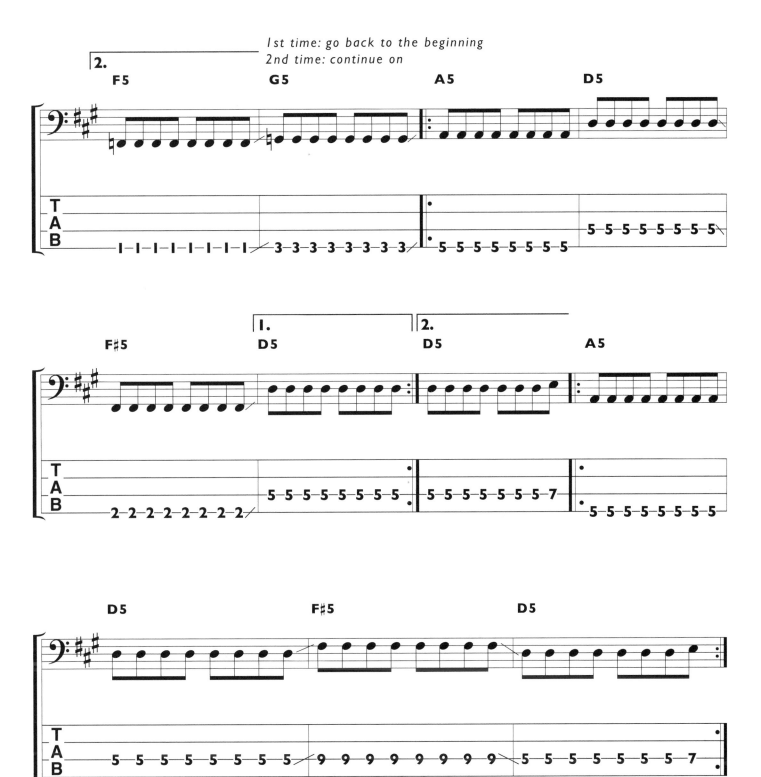

1st time: go back to the beginning
2nd time: continue on

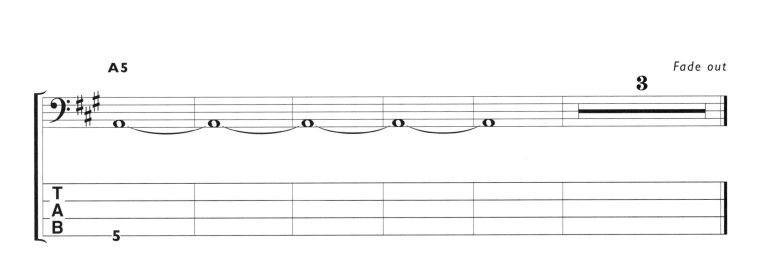

FUNKLY MY DEAR

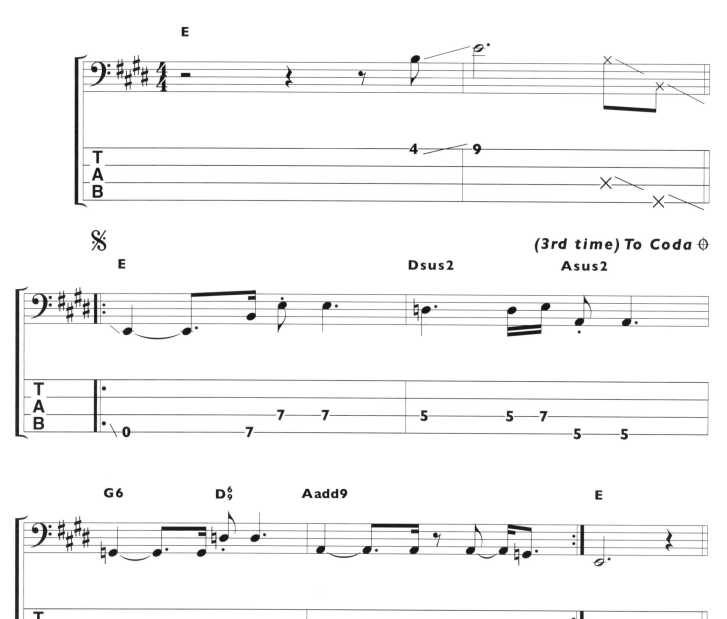

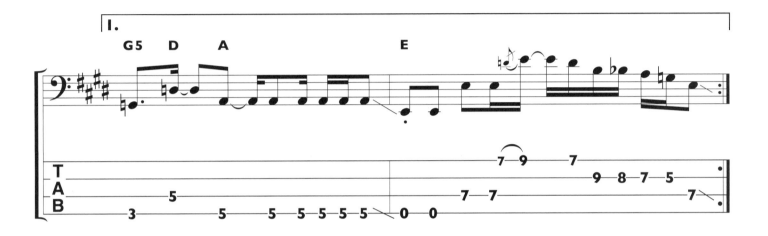

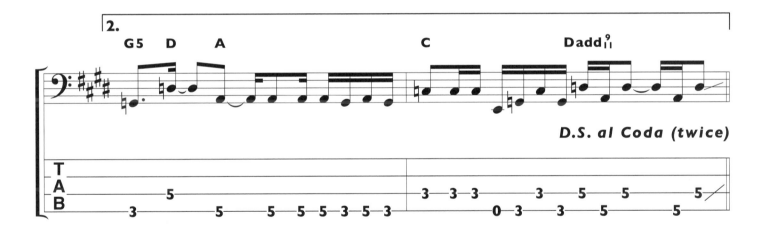

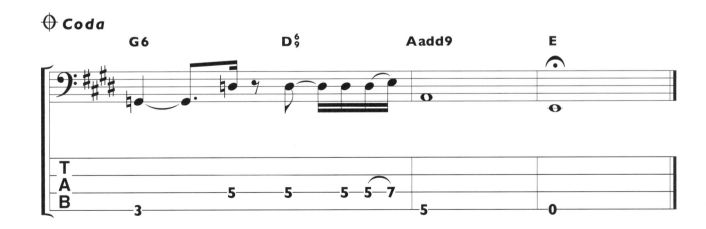

THAT WASN'T CHICKEN

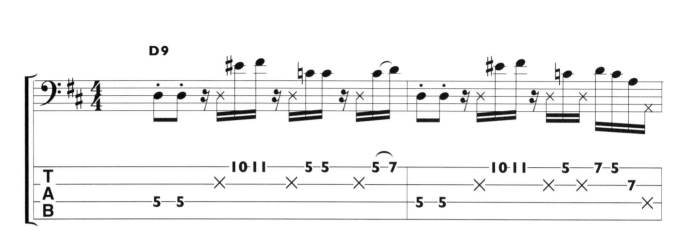

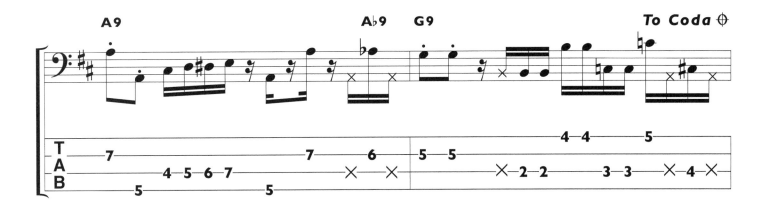

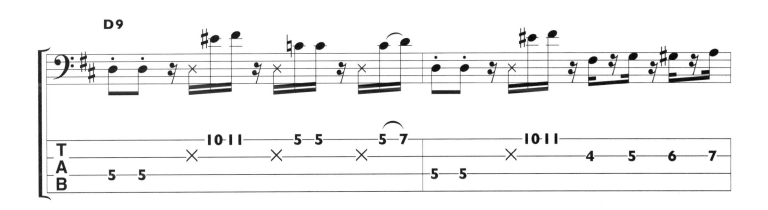

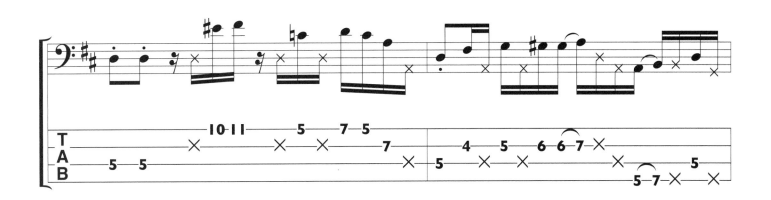

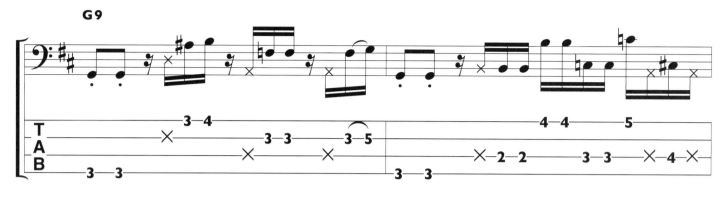

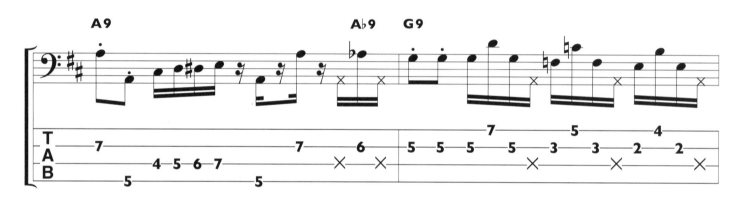

BONUS SONGS

CD 2
TRACK I

THE HOUSE OF THE RISING SUN

TRACK 2
Backing Track

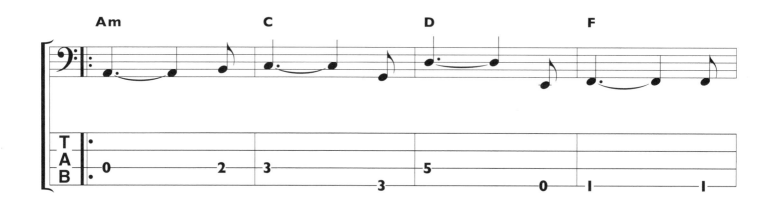

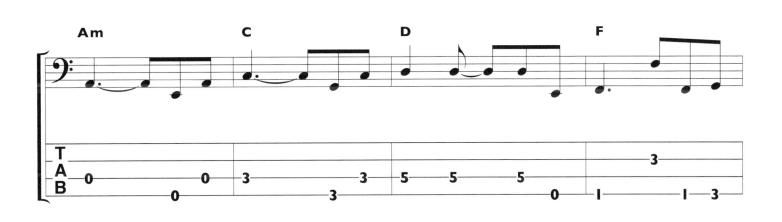
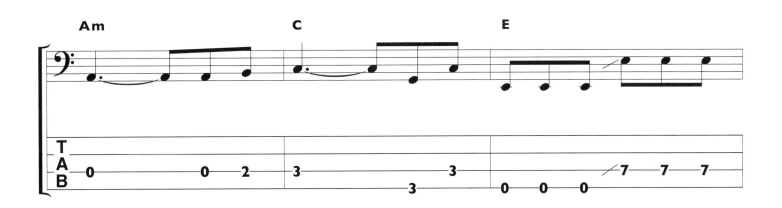

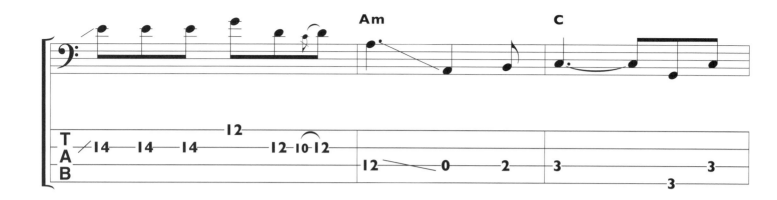

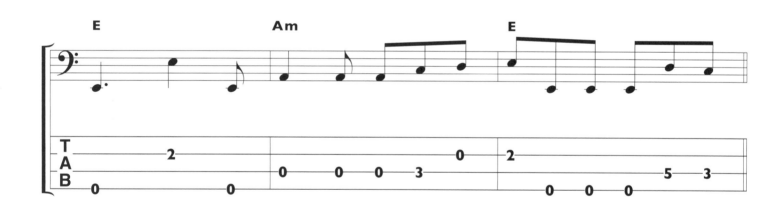

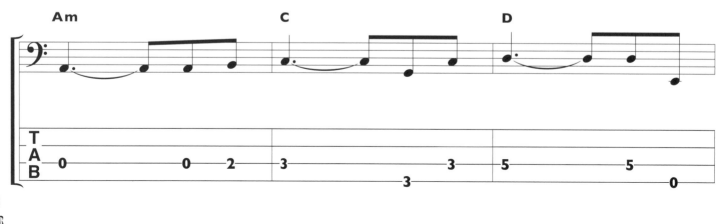

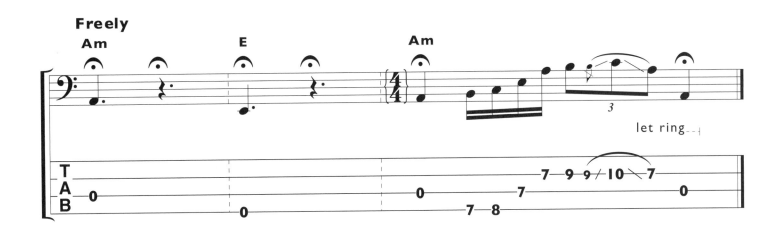

CD 2
TRACK 3

I AIN'T GOT NOBODY

TRACK 4
Backing Track

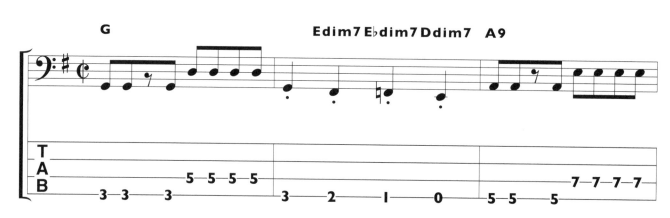

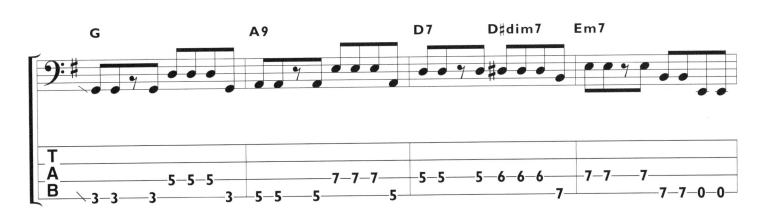

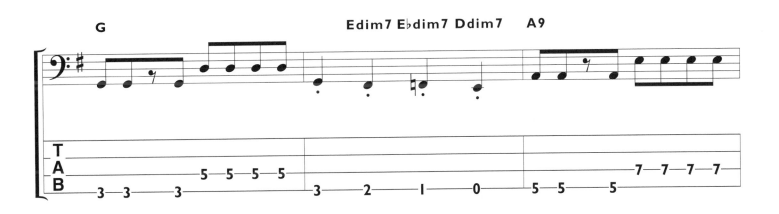

Edim7 E♭dim7 Ddim7

A9   D7

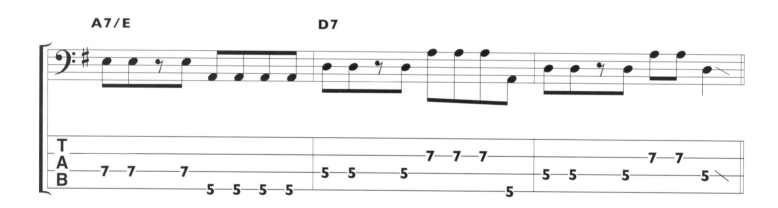

A7/E   D7

G7   C

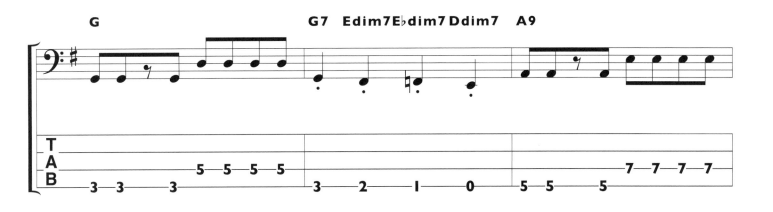

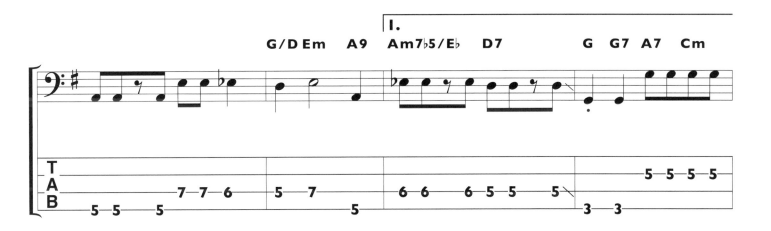

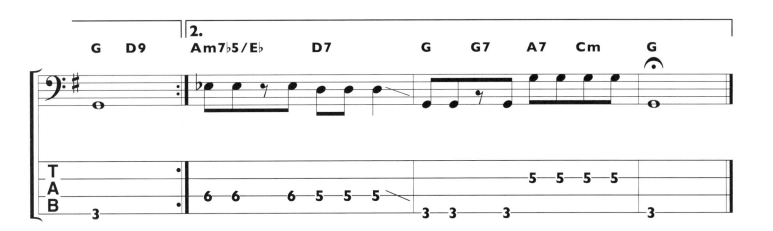

CD 2
TRACK 5

C.C. RIDER

TRACK 6
Backing Track

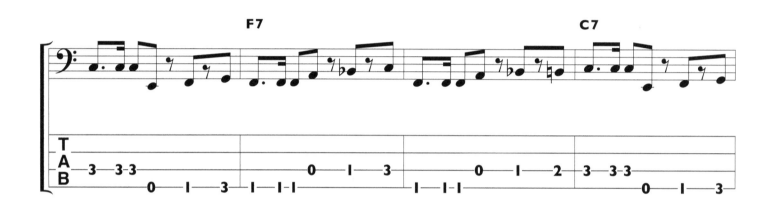

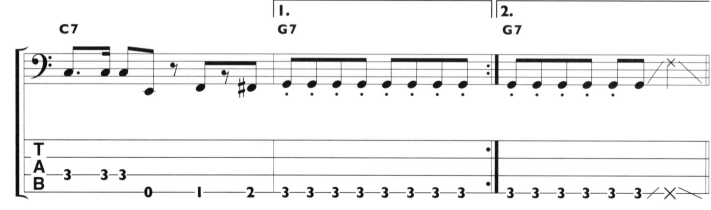

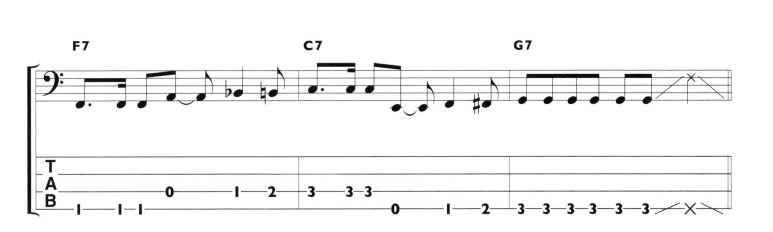

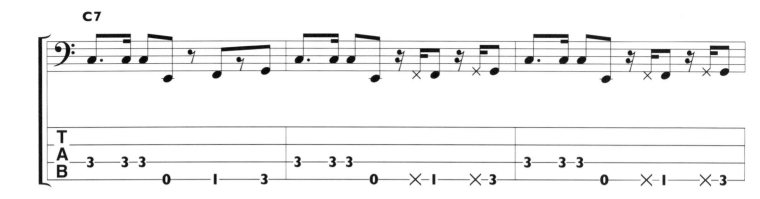

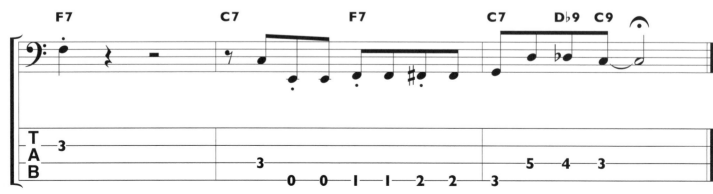

ST. JAMES INFIRMARY

CD 2
TRACK 7

TRACK 8
Backing Track

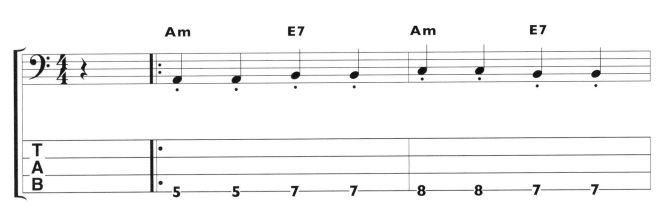

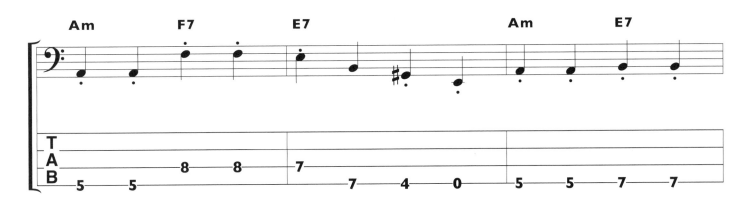

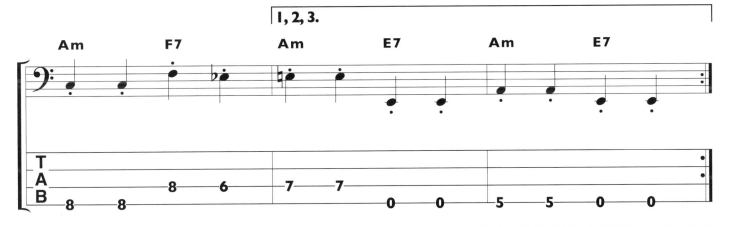

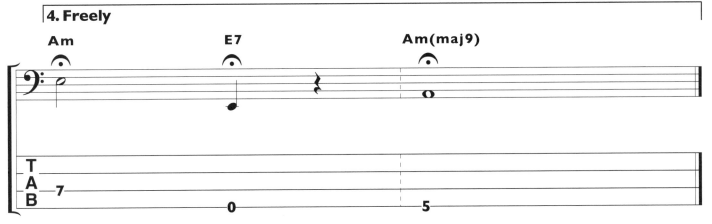

CD 2
TRACK 9

THIS TRAIN

TRACK 10
Backing Track

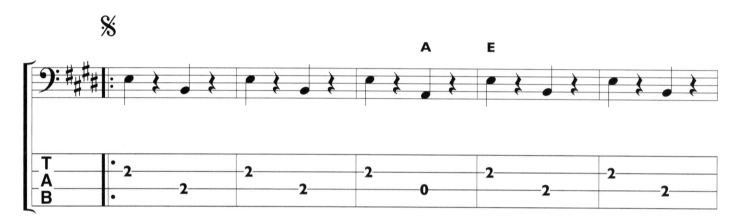

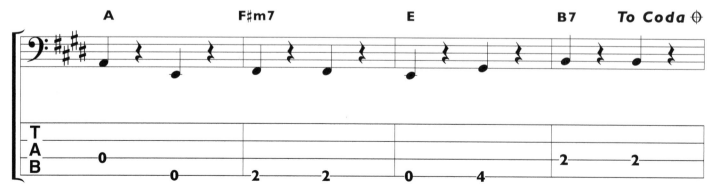

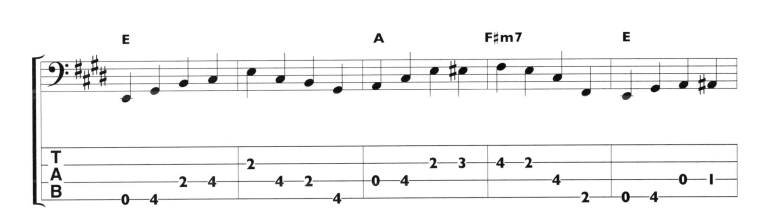

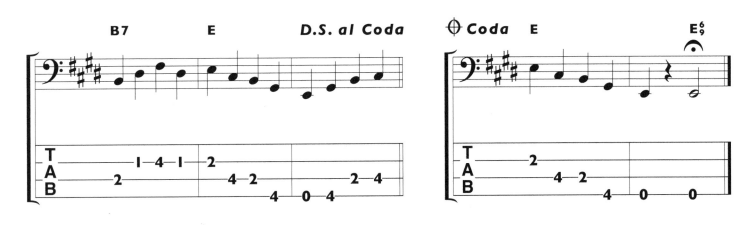
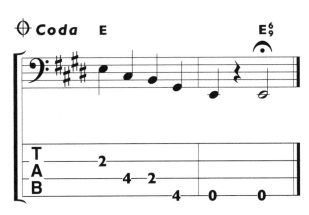

Bass tablature is a four-line staff that graphically represents the bass fingerboard. By placing a number on the appropriate line, the string and fret of any note can be indicated. The number 0 represents an open string. *For example:*

3rd string, 3rd fret   *4th string, open*

SLIDE (NOT RESTRUCK)
Strike the first note and then slide the same fret-hand finger up or down to the second note.

SLIDE (WITH RESTRIKE)
Same as previous slide, except the second note is struck.

SLIDE
Slide up to the note indicated from a few notes below.

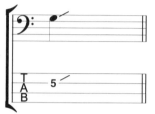

SLIDE
Strike the note indicated and slide up an indefinite number of frets.

HAMMER-ON
Strike the first (lower) note with one finger, then sound the higher note (on the same string) with another finger by fretting it without picking.

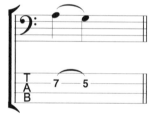

PULL-OFF
Place both fingers on the notes to be sounded. Strike the first note and without picking, pull the finger off to sound the second lower note.

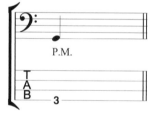

PALM-MUTE
The note is partially muted by the pick hand lightly touching the string(s) just before the bridge.

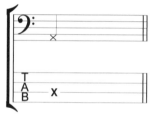

MUFFLED STRINGS
A percussive sound is produced by laying the hand across the string(s) without depressing it to the fretboard.

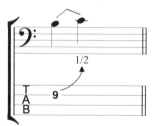

BEND (HALF-STEP)
Strike the note and bend up to a semi-tone (half-step).

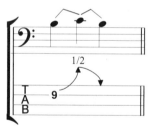

BEND & RELEASE
Strike the note and bend up as indicated, then release back to the original note.

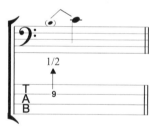

PRE-BEND
Bend the note as indicated then strike it.

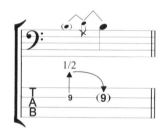

PRE-BEND & RELEASE
Bend the note as indicated. Strike it and release the note back to the original pitch.

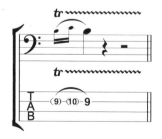

TRILLS
Very rapidly alternate between the notes indicated by continuously hammering on and pulling off.

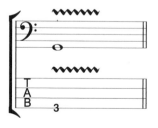

VIBRATO
The string is vibrated by rapidly bending and releasing the note with the fretting hand.

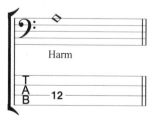

NATURAL HARMONIC
Strike the note while the fret hand lightly touches the string directly over the fret indicated.

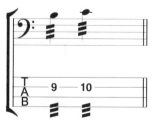

TREMOLO PICKING
The note is picked as rapidly and continuously as possible.

NOTE The speed of any bend is indicated by the music notation and tempo.